THE
SOLE TRADER
QUICK START
HANDBOOK

SUE HUNTER

First published in 2010 by dash house

ch

dash house

PO Box 394

Brockenhurst

Hants

SO41 1BP

www.dashhousepublishing.co.uk

Cover and book design by RULER

www.thisisruler.net

ISBN 978 0 9567357 1 3

A catalogue record of this book is available from the British Library

Printed and bound in Great Britain by Lightning Source UK Ltd

CONTENTS

Thanks to:

John, David and Angela

for their encouragement and practical help.

Also to Nick James – my favourite accountant.

INTRODUCTION

Sole trader, also sometimes known as sole proprietor or sole operator, is the legal status that is the most popular and straightforward form for start up businesses. The legal and accounting requirements for a sole trader are relatively simple and as a sole trader you will have complete control over your business.
In fact – you are the business. You will be responsible for all the debts but also take all the profits.

Often, the problem with doing something new is knowing where to start. You may have an idea of where you want to go but not how to get there. Initially there seems so much to sort out that you may never get past the thinking stage. This book aims to help you work through the initial stages of starting your own business so that you give yourself a fighting chance of succeeding and growing.

As a sole trader the success or failure of your business rests with you and that is why, in Chapter One, you are asked to assess you own skills and abilities and start a development plan for yourself and your business. Be honest concerning your motivations for wanting to be self-employed as unless you are clear about these, and satisfy yourself that they are sound, you will find it difficult to keep going when times get difficult. You must motivate yourself and don't let others put you off – rather, become more determined to succeed.

Chapters 2 and 3 talk about how to find customers who are willing to buy your product or service and how to let them know you are 'out there' and what you have to offer. Market Research is about finding out as much as possible about your customers so that you can tailor your product and services to their needs. It will also provide you with information about what form of advertising or promotions will attract their attention and encourage them to buy from you rather than a competitor. Marketing builds on this, as you will use the information to create an image that will attract your particular customers. A marketing opportunity will be created any time a potential customer sees you, reads about you, hears about you or interacts with you. On these occasions they will either be attracted by what they experience or will be turned off. You need to make sure that it's not the latter.

Chapters 4 and 5 cover the financial aspects of running a business and the records you should keep in order to retain control of your money. Making a profit is all about balancing your costs against your income from sales. You need to know something about the way different costs affect your profitability in order to be able to work out when you are likely to start making some profit. Taking time to estimate when you will have to meet certain costs, and when you can expect income from sales to be received, will provide you with the information you need for your cashflow. We work through an example of a cashflow in chapter 4 and look at how many sales you need to make in order to start making a profit. In chapter 5 we look at the records to keep for tax purposes and for monitoring how your business is performing against your estimates. Some examples of these are provided.

The final chapter looks at the business plan and gives an outline of a simple example. If you need to apply for a loan or other finance for your business you will need a business plan to submit with your application to reassure the prospective funder that you have a sound business idea which will provide them with a good return on their investment in you. However, even if you do not intend to seek outside funding, you should still write a business plan as this will enable you to cement in your own mind exactly what you are trying to achieve and how you plan to do it. It will help you bring together the different activities so that they take place at the right time and so you can afford to do them when you planned. If at any time your business is struggling then you can turn to your business plan and work out what's different and why you are not performing as planned. Your plan could help guide you to do the right things to bring your business back into line.

What you probably don't realise at the outset is how exciting having your own business can be. It will give you a real sense of achievement and, if you do it right, can provide for you and your family. Remember, you don't have to do everything at once. Just start with what you are able to manage now and tackle the other areas as soon as you feel confident to do so.

1

IT'S

ALL

ABOUT

YOU

1.0 IT'S ALL ABOUT YOU

Deciding to work for yourself rather than for someone else could be a turning point in your life. Your reasons for this will be personal and may be a mix of:

- Believing that you can do something better than others.
- Wanting the independence to be creative in your own time and in your own way.
- Relishing the challenge of establishing a profitable business.
- Believing you can make more money working for yourself.

These are good reasons for becoming self-employed, as they suggest that you are motivated by personal ambition and belief in yourself and it is these qualities which will sustain you through difficult times. Self-employment is not an easy option, so be aware of all the other tasks you will need to do apart from your main area of business. If you are not organised and focused on your business it will be easy to get in a muddle. Do a little planning, try some selling, keep an eye on the finances, take it easy and keep control. Learn as you go and you and your business can develop together.

There is one quality that you must develop in

order to make a success of your business – business acumen. Acumen refers to your ability to make good judgements and decisions based on your knowledge. To develop this you must start behaving and thinking like a business person rather than whoever you are to family and friends. At first it might feel a bit like developing a split personality – but gradually as you carry out your business it will become more natural. Learn about business terminology and try to understand why certain things, like business plans and market research, are important. Once you understand how it all fits into your business, your ability to make good judgements and sound business decisions will improve – and so will your chances of success.

You may have been thinking about it for sometime but, even so, probably wouldn't make the leap into self-employment without some additional stimulus. So maybe you've been overlooked for promotion at work or been made redundant; or perhaps you now have a partner and/or family to support and want a better life for them. You may have some other prompt which tells you 'now is the right time to do this'. If it feels like the right time, then it probably is – so let's get going.

1.1 <u>PERSONAL TOOLKIT</u>

As a sole trader you are your business. So, developing your business will mean developing yourself. Just think for a moment what you could offer that people will pay good money for. This could be:

- A particular skill because you are naturally talented or because you have trained or worked hard and developed a skill.
- Knowledge that you have acquired through experience or study.

I would like to be able to make this list a lot longer but when you think about it these are what it comes down to in the end – skills or knowledge. These are what you must acquire in abundance if you want to be successful in business. It could be that you have a trade skill or your particular skill may be in organising other people to work as a team, or your knowledge could be about something quite limited, such as a particular piece of machinery or equipment. That doesn't matter, just so long as you recognise where and how you can use these attributes in business. So, you might be starting very small. Match your business with your capabilities to start with – but as you do business your personal toolkit of knowledge and skills will develop and grow. As it does so, so can your business develop and grow too. Right now you might not know what you are capable of achieving, because it's not until you have some success under your belt that you will improve your self-confidence, which in turn will allow you to try new things. So, the idea is to use what you're good at now to start your business but be aware of what you need to develop to grow your business.

Work through the 'Personal Toolkit' checklist at Table 1 (T. 1) at the end of this chapter to start you off. Try to answer each question honestly and assess what your level is for each area. In this way you will have a starting plan to work on. In the following section we talk about creating a Development Plan. Once you have assessed your various skills and abilities, you should transfer any actions that you think you need to take to your Development Plan.

1.2 DON'T BE AFRAID OF SUCCESS

Even though you might be starting small this doesn't mean that you shouldn't have big ideas.

So, one of the first things you should do is to visualise your idea of success. What is your vision for your business and for yourself? Think of your longer term goals, how you would like life to be in 5 or 10 years' time and what you hope to have achieved by then. Then write yourself some targets – something to aim for along the way to guide you and to hang on to when times are difficult. If you know what you are trying to achieve, you will be able to decide what you need to do in order to achieve it.

Often the first step is the most difficult because it's this one that will take you outside of your comfort zone. Until now you might have had a limited circle of people to associate with everyday – your family, friends and a few work colleagues. Now, you're contemplating launching your business and that will mean a whole lot more, different, people to deal with. It could be a bit daunting. If this makes you feel nervous then be reassured that most people feel this way too. Whenever we step out of our comfort zones – the ones we are familiar with – it is natural to feel nervous. One of the most important qualities of successful business people is that they are brave – they are not afraid to try something new and put themselves 'out there' and say 'this is me, this is what I do, judge me on my performance'. Is this you? Could it be you?

Every successful business person will have had to take that 'first step' and then they will have proceeded to take another, and another, taking them out of their comfort zones and widening their horizons. This is what you must do – a step at a time.

1.3 DEVELOPMENT PLAN

Thinking about your motivations and abilities is one thing but acting upon them is quite another – and to help you do this you should write a simple 'Development Plan', covering both your personal development and your business development. No one else will do it for you – it's now down to you to move yourself and your ideas forward. An example of a plan you could use is at the end of this chapter. (See T.2). You'll see that it has a section for you to write down your goals and, underneath each goal, other sections for you to write the steps to show how you will achieve them. The 'how' you will do it is very important as this is what really requires the thought. Be realistic as to the timescale as well – don't give yourself too long as it may drag on, but allow yourself sufficient time to achieve your goals. Both goals and steps might refer to personal challenges or business targets. For example, a personal goal might be to achieve a particular qualification by the end of the year, and the steps might be to study for 15 hrs per week in preparation for this. A purely business target might be to launch your website and the steps could be finding someone to design it for you and a company to host it. Finally, put a big tick in the right-hand column when you have completed the activity. Some examples of goals and steps are given in this Table but, of course, you must create your own version of this.

Your development plan should be your kick-start to doing business but don't stew over it for too long and use planning as an excuse not to do anything practical. You should use it as a tool to stimulate your ideas and then update and amend it as you achieve actions and develop both yourself and your business. You need to start achieving something fairly early on, however, otherwise you will be slow to gather confidence in you ability to do business and may never get past the planning stage.

1.4 TURNING SKILLS AND KNOWLEDGE INTO BUSINESS

Your personal readiness to become self-employed is one half of the picture; the other half is whether or not you have a good business idea; one that will make you a living and help you achieve your ambitions. This is all about finding a gap in the market.

If you're going to offer something that other people already provide then you will need to do it 'better' than the others in order to gain customers. In the next chapter we talk about understanding what customers value and it is through understanding this that you will know how to do it better. One customer or set of customers might demand a painstaking high quality service but another might want a 'get it done quickly please' service. If you can find out what customers require and can provide this, then you have the makings of a business. The gap in the market might be that you find a group of customers that want 'it' done differently to what's already on offer. If so, do it differently. Do it better.

So a 'gap in the market' is something – a service or a product – that customers need, want, or would like to have that isn't currently being provided satisfactorily. Here are some reasons why there might be a gap – and where there could be an opportunity for you.

- <u>Current trends are not being met.</u> For example organic food becomes popular and supermarkets are slow to react.
- <u>Current products or services are too expensive.</u> Can you do it cheaper?
- <u>People are bored with 'the same old thing' and want something new.</u> E.g. new styles, new activities, new food and so on.
- <u>New customers might be interested.</u> Can you make something that is currently sold to only one group of customers interesting to a new group?
- <u>Goods or services are not being sold in the way customers want.</u> E.g. 'I want to buy on-line, but can't' or ' I want this service in my home but can only get it in town'.
- <u>Goods and services are not being delivered to the standards people want.</u> Know what these are – and deliver them.
- <u>Something is not available in a particular location.</u> Make it available.
- <u>You can provide something creative and different.</u> Quirky can be good – can you build a reputation for this?

Whatever you provide be aware that competitors may soon catch on and want to do the same, for example, the supermarkets now sell organic fruit and vegetables at a cheaper price than perhaps you could offer. So you must always think to the future and try to estimate how long your advantage will last and what you can do to protect it. You may, for example, develop a strong brand or you may quickly develop a group of loyal customers who will choose you as the preferred provider even when competitors knock at their door. The secret to success here is to think about the next steps before your current sales start to fall-off. Always be aware that nothing stands still in business and you must keep apace with changes and the threat from competition, – in trends, in new technology as well as with other external influences, such as legislation, that could affect your business.

1.5 <u>SOURCES OF ADVICE AND SUPPORT</u>

You may now be at a stage where you have a good idea of what you need to do in order to get started but don't quite know how to go about achieving it. You may need to go on a course, you may need finance or just want to learn about a particular aspect of business. There are many organisations around who will help you with advice and support. Some of these are listed at the end of this chapter (R. 1) together with web site addresses for you to find out more.

1.6 PERSONAL DEBT AND ATTITUDES TO SPENDING

There is one more area we need to cover before moving on to the next topic and that is personal debt. If you have high levels of debt which you are not managing to repay adequately, then, more than likely, you will have a poor personal credit rating. This in turn will mean that potential funders will be reluctant to lend you money or invest in your business because the way you manage your personal debt is a reflection of the way you will manage your business finances. When you apply for a loan for your business, whether from a bank or other organisation, they will run a credit check on you. If your rating is poor they will not provide finance as the likelihood is you won't repay it!

It is worth running your own personal credit check, whether or not you have a lot of debt, because other things can influence your rating. For example, your rating will be adversely affected if you are not registered on the electoral roll, (register on www.aboutmyvote.co.uk) or if you have moved house often, (register all your accounts and bills to the address you give on the electoral roll and give a landline telephone number rather than just a mobile). Also, having debt in itself is not a bad thing, in fact, in terms of your credit rating it is likely to be a positive if you are repaying on time, as it shows you are able to manage finances. So, deal with your debt now and negotiate to make some repayments to your creditors. For further information see: www.learnmoney.co.uk or seek advice from your local Citizens Advice Bureau. Two credit reference agencies you could check your rating with are:

• Experian
Telephone 08444 818000
www.experian.co.uk

• Equifax
Telephone 03301 000180
www.equifax.co.uk

You will need to provide your address history for the past 6 years.

T.1 PERSONAL TOOLKIT (TABLE)

Think which areas will be most important for you to be proficient in and prioritise those. Give them a priority number – and use this information to move yourself a step forward.

DO I HAVE THE SKILLS I NEED TO GET ME STARTED?	Yes / No	If No, what am I going to do about it?	Priority Number	Put on Development Plan?
Written skills (letters, advertising, forms etc)				
Spoken skills (speaking to customers, business people etc)				
Trade / professional knowledge or qualifications				
Money management (budgeting, finances etc)				
Self-organisation (time-keeping, paperwork etc)				
Coping with difficult situations. (Can I handle setbacks and difficult customers?)				
Planning (Am I used to planning for the future?)				
Using IT (email, letters, internet, databases)				
Willingness to try new things and experiment. (Will I be able to step outside my comfort zone?)				

DEVELOPMENT PLAN FOR
T.2 ## SAM'S VIEW PHOTO AND VIDEO (TABLE)

Year 1 aims:

- To have between 8-10 regular customers in the London area
- To have a turnover of about £50,000
- To buy a Nikon D700 camera & AF-S 16-35mm Lens

Sam's View Photo and Video: 31 March 2011 – 31 December 2011		
GOAL AND STEPS	Date to achieve	Done
1. Get x qualification	31 JUL 2011	
1.1 Study 3 hours per day for 5 days per week	Apr – 31 Jul	
1.2 Register for exam	5 Jun	
1.3 Submit portfolio	30 Jun	
2. To develop an electronic portfolio of my work to send to customers	1 SEP 2011	
2.1 Edit all photos	15-22 Jun	
2.2 Choose 2 videos to include	22-25 Jun	
2.3 Design layouts	1-31 Jul	
3. Contact all theatres and arts venues in London area	1 OCT 2011	
3.1 Find names and contact details for all venues	1 Sep	
3.2 Research styles and brands of each venue	1-14 Sep	
3.3 Send portfolio to each venue with customised covering letter	15-30 Sep	

SOURCES OF ADVICE
R.1 **AND SUPPORT (REFERENCE)**

Advertising Standards
Authority (ASA)
Regulates UK advertising
across all media,
including TV, internet,
sales promotions and
direct marketing.
www.asa.org

British Chambers of
Commerce
Offers advice and
training and run regular
networking events for
business owners.
www.britishchambers.
org.uk/find-your-local-
chambers

Business Link
Offers free advice and
support services online.
www.businesslink.gov.uk

Funderfinder
Provides software to help
you search for available
funds.
www.funderfinder.org.uk

Health and Safety
Executive
Offers advice and
guidance on all matters
to do with health and
safety at work.
www.hse.gov.uk

HM Revenue and Customs
Offer tax and financial
advice and guides online.
www.hmrc.gov.uk

Learndirect
Publicly funded
e-learning, offering a
range of qualifications
but is particularly useful
for English, Maths and IT
learning.
www.learndirect.co.uk

Prince's Trust
Enterprise training,
financial support,
mentoring and on-line
guides for young people
aged 18-30.
www.princes-trust.org.uk

Shell Livewire
Business advice, funding and social networking for young entrepreneurs aged 16-30.
www.shell-livewire.org

Trade Association Forum
Allows you to search for your trade association and holds discussion forums on-line to do with various aspects of business.
www.taforum.org.uk

UK Trade and Investment
Gives guidance to companies that intend to or are already exporting.
www.ukti.gov.uk/export.html

Unltd
Supports social entrepreneurs through funding and a range of resources and information.
www.unltd.org.uk

Young Foundation
Supports social entrepreneurs through research, discussion and investment.
www.youngfoundation.org

2

MARKET
RESEARCH

2.0 <u>MARKET RESEARCH</u>

What are the most important areas you should concentrate on when setting up in business? Is it the finances and the cashflow, or is it marketing and advertising, or perhaps efficient delivery and supply? These are all very relevant and during the course of this book you will find out why they are important. However, let's just think for a moment about what 'doing business' is all about.

Doing business is about:

• Being able to produce or provide something that people (your customers) need, want, or would like to have.

Fairly simple – but not the full story –

• Providing something that customers would like to have and be willing to pay for.

Getting closer –

• Providing something that customers would be willing to pay for and which you could provide and make a profit...

...after all, you need to make a living out of business- and hopefully a good one.

So putting it all together. 'Doing business is about providing something to customers at a profit.' The most important aspect of your business – of any business – will be your customers. Don't forget this! This is where your business starts. Without customers who are willing to pay for your product or service you have no business, however good your idea. Without customers you'll not have any finances to manage; you'll have no one to deliver your goods and services to, or to take an interest in your advertising.

Knowing about your customers, gathering information about them and analysing it is key. You must work out how you can use this information to persuade them to buy from you rather than another business. The whole way you do business – the prices you charge, the promises you make, the services you provide – is your complete 'offer' to customers. This is important because, unless you have invented something new, there will already be something 'out there' that is similar to your product or service. There may be lots of other people in the same trade or profession as you and many will be a lot more experienced and better skilled. There will probably be lots of like products on the market for people to spend their money on instead of buying yours. Many will have been around for years and will be real favourites.

2.1 SO WHY SHOULD PEOPLE COME TO YOU?

They will come to you if you can provide something that suits them better than what is already on the market. To know what might 'suit them better' you've got to learn about what customers value. Here are some things that might be important to different customers:

- Speedy Delivery.
- Good after-care service.
- Low price.
- High quality.
- Latest fashion.
- Personal attention.
- Expert knowledge.
- Efficiency.
- Quirkiness.

Often two or more of these are combined. For example, young girls might want the latest fashion but at an affordable (low) price. Mature ladies might want the latest fashion and be willing to pay a higher price providing they get individual attention. Retired homeowners might value a trades person who is willing to spend time with them and understand their problems, but busy professionals might want someone who is quick and efficient and who doesn't talk too much! Both might be willing to pay a little more if they get the sort of trades person they want.

So, you must find out about your customers and what they value and then decide how you can provide this. This is where you can win business from already established businesses. If you can find out more than they know about your customers' needs and then satisfy these needs better than your competitors, then you are in business! Market research, therefore, will not only involve finding out about your customers, but also about what your competitors are doing.

Your market research must not be a 'one-off' activity but is something that you should do on an ongoing basis. What is in fashion today might not be so tomorrow or something may happen in the wider world which will affect customer buying habits, or your competitors might do something that affects your business. You should make sure you keep up to date with these events. This 'knowing' is very important because it will help you keep one step ahead of your competitors.

2.2 BUSINESS MODEL

What you will end up with in business terms is a business model. Use what you know about your market to help you decide how best to create and deliver your product or service, what price(s) to charge, how to market your wares and your brand image. Thinking of it as a model is useful – it's the way you will do business in order to gain sales in your particular market. What do you need to focus on to succeed? For example, if you were promoting music gigs in a local area you might focus your business model around getting the best and most expensive DJs and latest sounds – but if this is costly and does not bring in the crowds, a reassessment might reveal that your business model should be around marketing and pricing which, if attractive to customers, will bring in the numbers which will in turn allow you to get the best DJs.

2.3 HOW TO DO MARKET RESEARCH

• PRIMARY RESEARCH
Getting Close To Your Customers

i) Current Customers
If you've been working in a particular business sector or trade for a while you may already know a lot about what customers want. Just by being around them you'll have observed what

they buy, what they ask for in particular, what extras they may want, what bugs them and so on. This is true whether you're a plumber or an accountant. You may not realise it but you will already have gathered useful information about your customers, so take a while to analyse this and work out what it's telling you about them. Draw a chart and use these headings.

- Customer Name and Location
- What I know about this customer
- What they bought and when
- How they heard about me
- Which aspects of my service/product do they like?
- What don't they like?
- Who else do they buy my type of service/product from –and what do they think about them?

If you don't know the answers already then ask them when you next see them, or phone and explain that you are doing some market research and could you ask them a few questions. More likely than not, they'll be flattered to be asked. Get as much information as you can.

ii) <u>New customers</u>
If you already have an idea of where to find your potential customers then it will be useful

to gather some more focused information about them through compiling a questionnaire and undertaking a survey. You might send this questionnaire to people but, even better, stand on the street or in a place where likely customers hang out and ask them the questions yourself. Yes, you have to be quite brave to do this and putting yourself and your business idea 'out there' is daunting at first, but you've got to get used to talking about your business to people; you must practice explaining what your business is all about and so doing market research in person is a good way to start.

An example of a questionnaire for someone wanting to find out if there is any market locally for gardening services is at T.3 at the end of this chapter. When you write your questionnaire be quite clear in your own mind exactly what it is you are trying to find out. Ask your questions in a logical order and make the wording of questions as precise and unambiguous as possible. You'll probably need to have a few goes at it before you have your final version, so try it out on friends or family, listen to their feedback and amend it.

iii) <u>Get a group together</u>
Rather than interviewing people individually, you might decide to get a group together and either

ask them questions or hand out the questionnaire and ask them to fill it in. You could specially arrange this and invite people along or, if your potential customers are likely to come from a group that you associate with regularly e.g. in the coffee bar at your local leisure centre, at a mother and toddlers group or in the pub, arrange to meet some of them and either hand out the questionnaire or ask them the questions. It might be an idea to check first with the management of the venue that they are happy for you to do this.

iv) <u>Get out there</u>

If you will be dealing with distributors and retailers rather than direct to end-users then try talking to them and find out as much as you can about the market. Visit trade fairs and exhibitions and talk to stall holders and customers – hand out your business cards, collect information and gather opinions. Prepare a few questions or topics beforehand that you would like to get feedback on.

v) <u>Other sources of information</u>

Although questionnaires can give you high quality information about your potential customer base, it will not give you much idea about your competitors or likely trends. For this you will need to do some secondary research.

- SECONDARY RESEARCH
Visit your local library

Anyone is entitled to visit public libraries and do research.

i) Local business information
Most libraries have copies of newspapers and magazines as well as local trade and business directories. Browse these to find out about your local competition – for example who's offering what, where they are advertising, what they are saying and charging.

ii) Local Trade Associations
Find out about your local trade association. Your library will keep a copy of the Directory of British Trade Associations. This will help you find out about what is going on in your business sector – for example if there are any local associations, newsletters, conferences, trade shows, exhibitions and so on. See also:
www.cbdresearch.com/DBA.htm

iii) Published market reports
You can find out about the size of your potential market, growth rates, trends and types of customers from specialist market reports. Ask you local library for any of the following:

- <u>Mintel</u>
For expert analysis.
www.mintel.co.uk

- <u>Datamonitor</u>
Covers business information across a range of industries. The service is subscription based but reports are available to buy online.
www.datamonitor.com

- <u>Key Note</u>
Gives a wide range of information about individual market sectors. Free executive summaries can be viewed on line.
www.keynote.co.uk

Information on your competition and what they are doing can be found in:

- <u>UK Kompass Register</u>
Information includes financial data, managers and company addresses.
www.kompass.co.uk/info/op_ukk_register.htm

- <u>Kelly's Business Directory</u>
Provides a list of suppliers and their contact details.
www.kellysearch.co.uk

- <u>Lexisnexis</u>
  Gives a range of articles about businesses across different sectors.
  www.lexisnexis.co.uk

Browsing these will help you further in building up an accurate picture of what's going on in your business sector. Most libraries stock a list of these reports and may be able to provide you with summaries or extracts. Some may let you use their online service to download and print some of the pages.

Browse the internet
Accessing published reports will usually cost you money. However, don't forget that you can browse the internet and find out useful information by researching social networking sites and see what people are talking about. Go onto blogs and microblogs such as Twitter that are tagged with key words relevant to your business. Join sites such as LinkedIn www.linkedin.com MySpace www.myspace.com or Facebook www.facebook.com to build up your personal profile, build up your network and connect with friends and other business people. When using these sites transparency and honesty are very important as you can build up a long tail! Likewise your competitors will have built their own 'tail' and this

might be very illuminating!

You can track topic trends on social networks and check for news about your sector by using Tweetdeck www.tweetdeck.com and Tweetscan www.tweetscan.com for checking what people are talking about on Twitter.

Use Technorati www.technorati.com and Google Blog Search http://blogsearch.google.com to search for key words and watch out for trends or news stories.

2.4 DON'T FORGET TO ANALYSE

There's plenty of information out there, but rather than waste lots of time browsing with no purpose make sure that you use your time most effectively. So, when doing market research make sure you know:

* What you want to find out
* What you have found out
* What you are going to do with the information!

Otherwise you may not have time to actually carry out your business.

2.5 <u>TEST MARKETING</u>

It would be a good idea if you could set up a limited test of the market before you launch wholeheartedly into business. The results of this will help you and potential funders determine whether or not there is a market for your product or service and let you refine your offer before you invest further time and money into the business. Some examples of test marketing might be:

- Put on a show or event – negotiate a venue, prepare and distribute leaflets and run the event. This will help you find out whether it would be as popular as you thought and discover potential problems and timings.
- Offer a limited service in a defined geographical area to determine interest and find out what other services customers may be need.
- Sell some of your product at a music festival, fete or on a market stall, give tasters, and get verbal feedback from customers.

If your test marketing is successful and indicates that there is a demand for your product or service then you should include the results in your business plan (See Chapter 6) as potential funders will be interested in this; however, if you receive disappointing results use this information to think about why this was the case and to plan what you will do about it.

2.6 THE SIZE OF YOUR MARKET

Your potential market must be big enough for you to be able to achieve your target earnings. If there are only a few customers likely to be interested in your product or service then you probably don't have a business. However, if your market research suggests that there are sufficient customers with similar needs and enough spending power for you to target and make a profit then you are in business. The value of your sales (quantity x price) must be high enough in order for you to surpass your breakeven position. (See Chapter 4).

T.3 EXAMPLE QUESTIONNAIRE FOR GARDENING SERVICES

- **Before you start**

  When you spot someone you want to interview, first catch his or her attention by saying, for example:

  'Excuse me sir/madam do you have a garden?' (Hopefully they will say 'yes') then say: 'Do you have a moment to answer a few questions to help me with my market research? I'm trying to find out what customers might like from a gardening service. It won't take more than 5 minutes. Thank you'.

  Whether they say 'Yes' or 'No' always be polite and thank them.

- **The Questions**

1	Have you used a gardening service in the last year or two?	
	Yes	If Yes, go immediately to 4.
	No	If No, go to 2.
2	Why haven't you used one?	
3	Is there anything that might make you consider using one in the future?	
	Yes	If Yes, record answer and go immediately to 7.
	No	If No, thank them for their time and finish.
4	What did you use them for?	
5	What did you like most about their service?	

6	What did you like least about their service?
7	Which services are you interested in? (Tick all that apply)
	Lawn mowing and care
	Planting
	Advice on plant selection
	Garden design
	Path and driveway weeding
	Water features
	Garden tool sharpening service
	Any other?
8	How often would you use this service?
	Daily
	Weekly
	Once per season
9	How much would you be willing to pay for this service?
10	Where would you normally look to find out about a gardening service?
	Local newspaper
	Internet
	Shop boards
	Any other?

Thank you very much for your time. Here is my business card. May I have your contact details?

Name, telephone number, address, email

3

MARKETING

3.0 MARKETING

Once you have found out as much as you can about your target customers you can decide how best to promote your business to them. You should have a clear picture of who your typical customer or group of customers will be. If this isn't the case then you need to do further research. Analyse this information so that you can create a business offer that is uniquely relevant to them. Write down everything that you think is important to your customers and how you can promote your business so that your marketing materials show that you know what is important to them AND why they should buy from you. This is often referred to as 'selling the benefits' rather than just the features of a product.

3.1 'WHICH MEANS...'

For example, if you are setting up a tanning salon, the features of your offer are that customers will get an all-over tan without any sunbathing. But what will this mean to your typical customers who might be young females or males? It might mean that they will look good on holiday, which might mean they will have a holiday romance, which might mean they will find a lifelong partner –

or just have a great time and get lots of photos on Facebook for their friends to see! A good tan could boost their self-esteem. Imagine the kind of advertising you would use to promote this aspect of the benefits. How could you use the knowledge about your customers to make your 'offer' stand apart from your competitors?

If you were selling electric drills your market research might have told you that your main customers were family men. A drill will not only make a neat hole in the wall, but also will bring the customer satisfaction because it will mean he can build those long awaited bookshelves and sit in his favourite chair to admire his collection.

Before you start marketing, therefore, you must know what benefits will be important to your customers and then ensure that everything your business does shows that you understand your customers better than your competitors do and you can provide all the little extras that you know will mean a lot to your customers.

3.2 YOUR MARKETING PLAN

The best way to organise this is to set out a simple Marketing Plan. This should cover:

- Your target customers.
- What's important to them – common traits.
- How you will attract them.
- When you will do each activity.

You should plan what methods you will use and when you will use them. Also, ensure that you find out exactly what each will cost and budget for this. You should also keep a record of the response you get from each activity and how many customers it brings to your business and adjust your plan accordingly. This will help you avoid the pitfall of spending a lot of money on badly targeted marketing, instead you can spend on what works.

3.3 HOW TO REACH YOUR CUSTOMERS

Advertising is one form of marketing your business. It's the bit that usually costs you money. However, every time you interact with a customer or every time they hear about you or see you, there will be a marketing opportunity. This hopefully will be a positive experience for both you and your customer, but if you do not pay attention to your image at all times, then it may be a negative marketing experience and harm your business rather than benefit it.

So, marketing starts with deciding on what image you wish to present to customers and then ensuring that this is carried through to every aspect of your business – to your dress style or uniform, to your manner of dealing with customers, to your literature and marketing message, to the car you drive and the promises you make to customers. The total is known as your 'brand'. Your brand is your promise to your customers and it is a promise that you must live up to. Never over-promise and under-deliver, rather, promise what you know your customers want and then delight them by delivering an even better service. This is how you will be remembered and how you can gain competitive advantage over your competitors. It is an ongoing, ever present activity.

3.4 BUILDING CUSTOMER LOYALTY

Once you have customers you don't want to lose them! It is important to keep reminding them that you understand their needs and can offer them solutions to their problems. Your competitors will always be 'knocking at the door' so you must give your customers reasons why they should stay loyal to you. Don't let them forget why they bought from you in the first place and educate them about the benefits of buying from you through such things as newsletters, special offers, open days or competitions. Make your customers feel appreciated; that they are important. Thank them for their custom after each purchase, ask them if they would like advance information of special offers or new products and reward their loyalty through discounts and special deals. Ask for their feedback and let them know that their opinions count. Remember a satisfied current customer is more likely to buy from you than someone who has not bought before.

Loyal customers are often the source of new business so consider including a request on every invoice to the effect: 'If you like what we've provided please tell your friends about us. Thank you'.

As the boss of the business you can choose with whom you do business and, quite simply, if you do not like a customer you do not have to deal with them. Experience shows that 80% of your problems in business will be caused by 20% of your customers – so look after your good, loyal customers and politely distance yourself from your troublesome ones. This could save you a lot of grief!

3.5 ADVERTISING

From time to time you will need to pay for advertising but, before you do, decide exactly what you hope to achieve from this in order to get best value for your money. So, decide the purpose of the advertising before choosing the media and then decide which will help you best achieve your objectives.

Your market research should have given you a good idea of what specific media your target customers pay attention to – which papers and magazines they read, whether they read professional newsletters, how often they use the internet, what radio stations they listen to, what TV they watch, the type of mail they open and read, whether they look at notices in local shops etc. Lots of homes also receive local parish or community magazines which carry advertising for local businesses at very reasonable rates. Decide which media to use and when to do your marketing in order to reach the right people at the right time.

i) Keep it simple

You may decide that a simple one-page flyer is the best way to get your message to customers. A useful rule to follow when designing and writing this, as with most adverts, is know as AIDA:

A = Attention. What will grab the attention of your prospective customers? Make this stand out clearly and simply.

I = Interest. You've done your market research so you know what elements of your offer will be important to your customers. Stimulate their interest by mentioning a couple of them.

D = Desire. Remember, it's not really the features that you're selling, but the benefits 'which mean ...' that if they buy from you they will satisfy some desire. Show this desire being satisfied.

A = Action. What do you want to achieve as a result of the leaflet or advert? Do you want customers to phone, to look at your web site, visit your shop? Is there a coupon they should cut out and return for a special offer? Be clear about this.

Above all, don't forget that advertising is part of your overall brand. What general impression do you want to convey? Will it be classy? Will it be cheap and cheerful? Will it be knowledge based or perhaps reassure customers as to your technical competence? Think how you can carry this branding through to everything you do, say or write and use appropriate language and images to convey this.

ii) <u>Advertising Online</u>
Every businessman or woman should consider using the power of the internet to promote their business as this can be very cost effective. However, as with all marketing you must have a clear idea of what you hope to achieve. Some methods include:

- <u>Online directories</u> – even if your business only serves a local community, at the very least you should consider having your business details included in online directories, such as Thomson www.thomsonlocal.com or Yell www.yell.com.

- <u>Develop a website</u> – a website will give you the opportunity to promote your brand and show in words and pictures why customers should buy from you. It is your shop front and should communicate everything about your business concisely and attractively. Make it easy to find and, unless you are already adept, you should employ a professional to design and structure your web site and make sure it appeals to your target market. They could also help you with search engine optimisation and keywords to ensure that you will be high up on the search engine pages like Google and Yahoo.

- <u>Social Media Marketing</u> – sites such as Twitter are a great way to get your name out there on the internet. You have unlimited opportunities to post links to your website, blogs, articles and so on. Social media marketing is much more personality based and personal than printed marketing material. You can give your followers interesting, useful and well-timed material.

- <u>Pay-per-click</u> – allows you to place an advertisement on a search engine results page and only pay for the advert when someone clicks on it. You do have to pay up front for the keywords, however, and this can be expensive. There are a number of PPC service providers that you can choose to host your advertising, including Yell Direct, Google Adwords, Yahoo! and Facebook. There are also tools that you can use to generate keywords. One example is free from SEOBook tools.seobook.com/keyword-list.

iii) <u>Newsletters and eNewsletters</u>
If you are able to produce good standard written material then try creating a regular newsletter for your existing customers and to attract new ones. Your newsletter must not be waffle; it must

contain material that is of interest and value to your customers such as advice and information, special offers, competitions, news of events and new products or services. Look at it from the point of view of your target audience and imagine what would interest them.

Email newsletters could offer you the ability to track who opens your enewsletters, what links they click on and what content they read. They will allow you to measure how readers respond to your content. Make sure you give visitors to your website the opportunity to enter their email address to receive a free newsletter and advice and include this in all your publicity material.

iv) <u>Conversion rates</u>

Whichever advertising method you choose you should always measure the success and track what works and what doesn't work, otherwise you might be spending money uselessly. You could:

- Add a code into the advertisement that you ask customers to quote.
- Ask customers how they heard about you or where they saw your advert.
- Provide a hook that customers have to act on such as cutting out a voucher from an advertisement to receive a discount or free item.

Focus your future effort and expenditure on the most effective methods – and keep monitoring.

3.6 SALES TECHNIQUES

You must be able to explain your business offer to people and so you should practise your sales pitch – in front of a mirror or to family and friends – until you are confident. Use what you know about your customers to show them how buying from you will be a benefit to them. Have your information to hand:

- Know all the features of your product or service.
- Be able to explain simply the main benefits to customers.
- Answer any likely objections.
- Say why you are better than competitors.

Have all this information ready so you can give your sales pitch at an appropriate time and feel comfortable doing this. Do not use jargon which customers will not understand; rather, explain your business using language to suit your customers. Remember, listening to what the customer is telling you is more important than bombarding them with information.

3.7 SALES CHECKLIST

Here are some tips to help you with the sales process:

- <u>First Impressions</u> – be on time, dress for the occasion, smile, greet and make eye contact.

- <u>Build Rapport</u> – everyone likes to talk about the weather – mention it! Compliment customers e.g. you have a lovely home. People then will think you are similar to them and have the same tastes or styles.

- <u>Questioning</u> – ask open questions, i.e. ones which will require them to say more than a 'Yes' or 'No', e.g. rather than asking 'Do you like this kind of music?' you could ask ' What music do you listen to?' Open questions start with 'What' Which' 'When' 'How' etc
Note: Yes, you are 'selling' but part of this is listening to what people are telling you. In fact, you should listen more than you talk. Don't forget!

- <u>Presentation</u> – listening will help you get a feel for what is particularly important to your customer, then you can say what your product or service will do for them, e.g. save them time, make them look good.

- <u>Listen for buying signals</u> – a customer may make up their mind to buy before you've finished your pitch! Listen for these 'buying signals', e.g. they may say 'When can you deliver by?' or ' I like the blue one'. If they do then stop 'selling' and close the deal!

- <u>Closing</u> – Once you've been chatting for a while you should test whether you have made the sale by attempting a trial close. Close the deal by asking for the business, for example by saying 'How many would you like?' or 'Shall I wrap that one for you?'

- <u>Thanks and Follow-up</u> – thank them for the business. Ask for a referral or think of another way to achieve follow-on business from your current customer.

3.8 <u>CUSTOMER CARE</u>

There are two rules to good customer service:

i) The customer is always right.
ii) When you believe the customer is wrong, refer to Rule 1…

Studies show that while a customer who has had a good experience will tell one person about it, a customer who has had a bad experience will tell nine – or if it gets discussed online – many more!

If a customer complains about your product or service make every effort to deal with it quickly and politely. Complaints can help you pinpoint problems with your business and so it is important to take notice of them and act upon them. Your policy should be to:

- Take a note of the complaint.
- Apologise for the problem.
- Investigate it fully.
- Offer a replacement product, a refund or credit note.
- Make a follow-up call or letter to ensure that the customer is now satisfied.

Your customers have a number of legal rights that you should be aware of. These rights apply whether they bought something in a shop, by mail order or online:

- If you sell a product that is faulty the customer is entitled to a full refund.
- If a service is not provided with reasonable care and skill, within an agreed timescale and for an

agreed price, customers can ask for a full or part refund.
- If you sell goods by phone, mail order or over the internet, customers have the right to a 'cooling-off period' during which they are entitled to change their minds and cancel the order.

The Office of Fair Trading provides guidance on customers' legal rights – www.oft.gov.uk.

Businesses that hold information on individuals must also comply with Data Protection Act 1988 – www.informationcommissioner.gov.uk.

All businesses have a duty to ensure their advertising is legal, decent, honest and truthful. You can get further details from the Committee of Advertising Practice – www.cap.org.uk.

3.9 DON'T FORGET - YOU LEAD YOUR BRAND

Marketing is all about getting your message out to your current customers and prospective customers. Advertising is one form of marketing but everything you do, say or write is part of your marketing and some of it will be planned and some unplanned. So, you need to be aware that as a business you are in the public eye and try to make sure that your brand image is consistent.

Don't be afraid to talk about your business to people and don't be afraid to sell your business to customers. After all, if you have a good product or service to offer there are people out there who would welcome the opportunity to buy from you. Show them you know what they want and how you can provide it; in that way you'll be doing them and yourself a favour.

4

PRICING, BUDGETING AND CASHFLOW

4.0 <u>PRICING, BUDGETING AND CASHFLOW</u>

In Chapter 2 we learnt that 'Doing business is about providing something to customers at a profit'. Vital to this, of course, is having customers who are willing to pay for your goods or services, but another critical aspect is to control the costs so that you do actually make a profit. Your sales will bring in income at certain points throughout the year but you must ensure that you have sufficient money coming into the business at the right time in order to pay your bills. Calculating when, and from where, money will come into your business and when it will go out is what budgeting and cashflows are all about. Money flows are not something that just happen – you control them.

4.1 <u>SETTING A PRICE</u>

First, it is important that you set the right price for your goods or service. If you pitch your price too low you may not be covering all your costs and if you pitch it too high you may not get anyone to buy at the price.

i) <u>Cost Plus method</u>
This is where you work out all your costs and then add a percentage markup to allow for unforeseen expenses and to provide a profit. You must know your costs in order to make sure your price is

high enough to make a profit but your price also should reflect the value your customer places on your goods or service. If this value is less than what it costs you to provide the product or service, you don't have a business. If it is high you could be underselling your product if you base your price on cost plus a percentage profit. So to do this in isolation, ignoring your competitors' prices or how much your customers might pay, is not a good idea. Pricing your product or service too low is best avoided because raising prices later is difficult and may lose customers without good justification for this.

ii) Perceived value

Your market research will have given you a good idea of what prices your competitors are charging and this is the starting point for setting your own prices. Could you charge more by providing something that your customers value that is not offered by your competitors and does not cost you a lot to provide? Work out what your competitors do well and what they don't do so well – you could copy the better things and use what they don't do well to steal an advantage over them. For example, if they are unreliable make sure that you are reliable and promote that aspect in your advertising literature. What you are really setting a price to is your total 'offer' to customers – this is the sum of everything you are offering. This will include not only the basic product or service but all the additional benefits that you might include such as speedy delivery, excellent warranties, technical support, wide choice, personal service and so on. But these will only attract a higher selling price if they are important to your customers. This is the perceived value.

iii) <u>Undercutting</u>

Alternatively, you may decide to undercut your competitors and try to gain business that way. You might focus on keeping costs to the very minimum; your additional benefits to customers might be almost nil – and if your market research has shown that this is what your customers want, i.e. low price with few frills, then it could be the right option for you. However, be aware that:

- It might trigger price cutting by your competitors and a downward spiralling of prices in which no one wins and no profits are made.
- You must cover your costs and make a little extra to put back into the business.
- Low price might be associated with low quality in the mind of the customer and make it difficult for you to improve your image and increase prices later.

iv) <u>Discounting against a high price</u>

If you want to maintain your brand image as high quality / high price you could choose to compete by offering special price discounts or special promotions, whilst keeping the 'normal' price high. You could use this option to offset seasonal variations in the demand for your product or service or use it to win customers who normally use a cheaper competitor.

You might need to experiment with prices and see what effect lowering or raising the price has on your sales. Raising your price could lead to a fall in sales volume and lowering them could increase sales – but by how much? Again, the answer is in knowing your customers and how they will respond to price changes.

4.2 <u>COSTS</u>

You will not know whether a change in price means bigger profits until you have included an analysis of costs in your reckoning.

All your costs relate to things that are going on in your business. These costs fall into three categories – start-up costs, variable costs and fixed costs.

i) <u>Start-up costs</u>

At the outset, work out what you think your start up costs will be. So, for example, these may include the purchase of equipment or some form of transport, initial supply of raw materials or purchase of premises. Make a list of these costs and be as accurate as possible; do your research to make sure you know what you will have to pay and whether this will be 'up-front' or whether you can negotiate spreading the cost throughout the year. Make a note of when you will have to make the payments. This will help you determine whether you need additional finance to get you going.

ii) <u>Variable costs</u>

If you have to buy goods, materials and/or services in order to make sales, these purchases, or costs, will vary according to the volume of business you do. For example, if you make and sell an evening dress for £100 but the cost of the material, thread and other decoration was £50 then the variable cost of your sales will be £50 per £100 of sales. Put another way, the variable cost of your sales will be 50% of your sales value.

Variable costs might also include contract labour or casual labour needed either to produce the goods or fulfil services or delivery costs.

Once you begin trading you will have to meet these costs. Calculating them, therefore, means firstly estimating your sales.

iii) <u>Fixed costs</u>

Once you have done most of your research for your business you will need to decide on your business model, essentially:

- How you are going to make your product or deliver your service.
- Where you are going to operate from.
- How you will get your product or service to market.

Setting up your business, even without any sales, will mean that you will incur some ongoing costs:

- Advertising and Promotion.
- Vehicle Maintenance.
- Printing, Postage, Stationery.
- Phones, including mobile.
- Equipment costs.
- Utilities e.g. heating, lighting.
- Rent and rates.
- IT costs.
- Interest on loans and overdraft.
- Professional fees.

Note that none of these costs are 'money earners', that is they are not directly related to your making or selling the product or service and will not necessarily result in sales. For this reason they are known as 'overheads' (or fixed costs). It is important that you keep a tight control of these and make sure that expenditure is necessary before committing yourself. From the outset you should estimate how much you plan to spend in each area and when you plan to spend it. Decide on a budget for each and then try to stick to it. Group your main area of expenditure under budget headings. These amounts will also be included in your cashflow.

Your own money – personal drawings

What you take out of the business as your pay (personal drawings) will be part of your fixed expenses and you should work out how much you will need each month to live on. This is called your Personal Survival Income (PSI) and you should include everything you need for yourself and your dependants including such things as all household bills, entertainment, clothing, food etc. Once you have estimated your total monthly financial needs you should then deduct from this total any income you receive from other sources. The result will be what you need to make from your business in order to meet your personal living requirements. These monthly amounts will be included in your cashflow as 'drawings'. A blank template is included at the end of this chapter in T.4 for you to calculate your PSI.

4.3 ESTIMATING SALES

Once again, your market research should provide the information you require here. From your research you should have a good idea of the potential for sales and be able to make an estimate of how long it will take you to grow these sales. Do not make the mistake of just assuming that sales will be there, that people will automatically buy from you rather than someone else. When estimating your sales you should plan when to advertise and undertake other marketing and have targets which you plan to achieve as a result of these activities. You must think where your sales will come from and be confident that you will be able to manage the sales, i.e. deliver on time and deliver the service you promised. It is best to grow your business slowly, and learn about the problems and realities of producing and delivering a product or service before going after new business.

When estimating sales, work out how much business you think you can achieve in a typical week and estimate the value of this. As most businesses have good times and low, often due to seasonal fluctuations, also estimate what you think a good week would look like as well as a bad week. Take these amounts and multiply up to show estimated sales for a typical (average) month, a good month and a bad month.

What are the particular costs associated with delivering this volume of sales? Of course, your variable costs figure will be an estimation – it won't be precise – but that doesn't matter, just have a go at trying to work out all the costs involved.

Your fixed costs plus your variable costs gives you a figure for your total costs. This information, together with your sales estimates gives you the figures to plan your cashflow for the forthcoming year.

4.4 <u>CASHFLOW FORECASTING</u>

Cashflow forecast is an estimate of when you think you will receive cash into your business and when you will have to pay it out. It is important because it is the measure of your ability to pay your bills on a regular basis. It depends on the timing of the amounts of money flowing into and out of your business each week and month.

At the end of the chapter is an example of a completed cashflow which is explained below. To start with use a spreadsheet for your cashflow, but later you might consider using an accounting package such as **Money Manager** from Connect Software.

• <u>Cashflow for 'Sam's View' (See T.5)</u>
Sam is setting up as a freelance Video Photographer. He is going to focus on producing videos for Corporate Clients and Performing Artists. These are his two main income streams.

The cashflow has 12 columns, one for each month covering the first year of business. It also has a column labelled 'Pre Start' where Sam has worked out how much he will need in order to get started and to cover him until he is established. He is going to borrow £1500 from his mother and repay her over the year at £130/month which will give her some interest on the loan.

He is also going to put £1500 of his own money into the business. CASH IN is shown at the top of the page and CASH OUT is shown underneath this. The calculations showing whether Sam has more coming in than he has going out (Net Cash Flow) is shown in the third line from the bottom and opening and closing balances for each month are shown below these.

Under 'Sales' Sam estimates that income from corporate clients will fall significantly in January because of reduced business in December but income from performers will increase in January as a result of more business activity in December. Note that he estimates a month's lag between doing the work and getting paid.

You will see that he has calculated his monthly outgoings under his main budget headings shown in the left hand column. He plans occasionally to use the services of a contract photographer and these costs are shown under 'Casual labour'. His own drawings will vary according to profit made and his personal needs. He has also estimated the amount he will have to spend on supplies each month in order to fulfil the orders for the following month. He estimates that supplies will cost about 1/10th of the value of his sales.

The bottom line shows Sam that he is likely to be in deficit in the first few months of business and so he should arrange with his bank manager for an overdraft facility sufficient to see him through this period. By the end of the year, however, he estimates that business should have made a profit of £14,491 to carry forward to the next year.

4.5 MANAGING YOUR CASHFLOW

The secret to ensuring that you 'stay liquid', i.e. that you have sufficient cash to pay your debts when they are due is to keep control of your flows of cash into and out of the business. Some ways to manage these are:

i) <u>Set up your systems at the outset</u>
Prepare your budgets and cashflow forecast in advance of each year's trading and then during the year review your progress against your estimates on a regular basis – at least once per month. In your cashflow add another column to the right of each month where you can add in the actual figures for that month as and when you have them. Once you have this information you must use it to plan for the future and take any actions you need.

ii) <u>Control your income</u>

Be careful how much credit time you give to customers – allowing customers to pay sometime after they have received the goods or service will cost you money. Define your payment terms before they buy. These could be Cash with Order (CWO); Cash on Delivery (COD); payment after a certain period e.g. 7 days or 30 days. You could offer a discount for early payments or other incentives to encourage early or prompt payment. Also, consider exercising your right to charge a penalty interest for late payment.

If a customer is likely to buy a lot from you then make sure you check them out thoroughly before doing business. Do not assume they are credit worthy.

• Send out invoices promptly – do not be sloppy over this. Sending out invoices on time is critical to maintaining cashflow. Do not give customers the impression that it doesn't matter when they pay. Chase up overdue payments politely but firmly both in writing and by phone. Bank all cheques and cash immediately.

• Keep proper records – if you have a few major customers keep separate records for each, detailing: what you have sold to them, how much they owe and when they pay. Use this information to work out which are 'good' payers and which are poor and need watching.

iii) <u>Control your expenditure</u>

- Manage your suppliers – in all likelihood you will have a few key suppliers so try to arrange with these to be billed quarterly, rather than monthly for major expenditure. If this is not possible then negotiate the best deal you can and do not pay until you have to. You may also be able to negotiate discounts for certain purchases. Get to know your suppliers and establish a good working relationship so that you become a valued customer to them.

- Consider leasing rather than buying – rather than buying outright consider leasing cars, vans and office equipment which will help spread payments over the year.

iv) <u>Use your cashflow</u>

As you update your cashflow with actual figures you will need to adjust your future estimates in the light of what you are discovering, so your cashflow will be a dynamic document, something that you will use to decide whether your business is on track as planned or whether there are steps you should take to bring it back in line. For example, you may decide that you need to increase your overdraft for a period and arrange this with your bank manager or you may decide to bring forward an advertising campaign to boost sales. Alternatively, if you are doing better than planned you may decide to put some spare cash into a higher interest account or invest in short term investments. Your bank manager will be able to advise.

4.6 BREAKEVEN POINT

Your breakeven point is achieved when your sales income reaches the level at which it covers start up, variable costs, fixed costs and your personal survival income. Some businesses simply will never sell enough to make a profit – they will never reach their breakeven point – and so will fail right from the start. A simple calculation at the outset will give you a good indication of whether or not your business is ever likely to be profitable.

To calculate your breakeven point start with these 3 steps:

i) Decide what your 'unit' of sale will be
It could be one item of your product or one hour, or one day's worth, of your time if you're providing a service. Whatever you use you must be able to

put a sales value to it – let's say that one unit of your product might sell for £15.

ii) <u>Work out your variable costs to provide one unit</u>
Remember, these are costs related specifically to providing one unit of sale such as material, labour and delivery costs. In this example we'll say they are £10.

iii) <u>Work out your fixed monthly costs</u>
For example, rent, business rates, electricity, stationery and other business expenses, plus your personal survival income. Let's say these are £1,000 per month.

You will see from the above that each sale of £15 would make £5 (£15-£10) towards paying your fixed costs of £1,000 per month. If each sale contributes £5 toward your fixed costs then you would need to sell £1,000 ÷ 5 = 200 units per month in order to break even. This can be shown as the following formula. Breakeven point =

$$\frac{\text{fixed costs (per month)}}{\left(\begin{array}{ccc} \text{price of} & \_ & \text{average variable cost} \\ \text{1 unit} & & \text{of producing 1 unit} \end{array}\right)}$$

So, selling 200 units per month would enable you to break even in that month, however, you might aim to sell 500 units per month. Once you have the information from steps 1-3 above you can estimate whether your expected level of sales will produce a profit. Let's see how the above translates into a financial summary:

i) In one month you plan to sell 500 units at £15 each _____ £7,500

ii) Take away the variable costs of producing those sales, i.e. 500 x £10 _____ £5,000

iii) Which leaves a profit before fixed costs of 1/3rd of sales value (i.e. your variable costs are 2/3rd of the selling price) _____ £2,500

iv) Take away your fixed costs for one month _____ £1,000

v) Which leaves a profit of _____ £1,500

Try to get a feel for these figures and be aware of how your variable and fixed costs will affect your profitability. By doing this you will soon begin to understand how important it is to keep a tight control over your costs.

T.4 PERSONAL SURVIVAL INCOME

Use this form to work out what it costs you to live each month, then you will know how much money your business needs to make and what you will need to take in drawings each month.

Estimated monthly living costs	£ (n/a if none)
Rent / mortgages	£
Council tax	£
Electricity / gas / water bill	£
Food / household bills	£
Clothes	£
Car tax / maintenance	£

Car petrol / diesel		£
National insurance		£
Phone bills		£
Family expenditure (children / dependants)		£
Social life (meals out, drinks, clubs)		£
Holidays		£
Home entertainment		£
Subscriptions (magazines, gyms, leisure clubs)		£
Credit cards / other loan repayments		£
Savings plan		£
Dental / medical		£
Other (please state)		
A	ESTIMATED TOTAL MONTHLY LIVING COSTS	£
Estimated monthly income		£ (n/a if none)

Working tax credits	£
Income from partner / family members	£
Child benefit(s)	£
Pension / investment	£
Other (please state)	
B **ESTIMATED TOTAL MONTHLY INCOME**	£
SURVIVAL INCOME (DRAWINGS) NEEDED FROM BUSINESS [A-B]	£

T.5 EXAMPLE CASHFLOW

CASHFLOW FORECAST FOR 12 MONTHS ENDING 31 MAR 2011						
	Pre	Apr	May	Jun	Jul	Aug
	0	1	2	3	4	5
Quantity of sales						
Cash in						
Customers (corporate)		400	2000	2000	3000	3000
Customers (performers)				1000	1000	2000
Own funds	1500					
Personal loan	1500					
A TOTAL CASH IN	3000	400	2000	4000	5000	5000
Cash out						
Personal drawings		800	800	800	800	1500
Casual labour		100		200		300
Capital expenditure	1000					
Supplies	300	250	250	300	400	500
NHI (staff and personal)		12	12	12	12	12
Business rents and rates		120	120	120	120	120
Marketing and advertising	250	50	50	50	250	100
Services (electricity / gas / water)		15	15	15	15	15
Phone / phone bills	100	45	45	45	45	45
Business / Public liability insurance	395					
Car petrol / diesel		200	200	200	200	250
Car maintenance				60		
Loan repayments		130	130	130	130	130
Legal / professional				250		
Net VAT payments						
Other travel / subsistence			150		150	
B TOTAL CASH OUT	2045	1742	1792	2202	2142	2992
NET CASH FLOW IN / (OUT) [A-B]	955	-1342	208	798	1858	2008
OPENING BALANCE / (DEFICIT)	0	955	-387	-179	619	2477
CLOSING BALANCE / (DEFICIT)	955	-387	-179	619	2477	4485

BUSINESS NAME:			SAM'S VIEW PHOTO AND VIDEO				
Sep	Oct	Nov	Dec	Jan	Feb	Mar	TOTALS
6	7	8	9	10	11	12	
							0
3500	4000	3000	1000	1000	2000	3000	30400
1500	1500	2000	2000	3000	1000	2000	17000
							1500
							1500
5000	5000	6000	5000	4000	3000	5000	50400
1500	1500	2000	2000	2000	2000	2000	17700
300	300	600	300			100	2200
							1000
500	500	400	400	400	400	300	4900
12	12	12	12	12	12	12	144
120	120	120	120	120	120	120	1440
50	50	50	50	50	50	50	1100
15	15	15	15	15	15	15	180
45	45	45	45	45	45	45	640
							395
250	250	250	200	200	200	120	2520
60			60			60	240
130	130	130	130	130	130	130	1560
250			250				750
							0
150		150		150		150	900
3402	2942	3792	3602	3142	2992	3122	34909
1598	2058	2208	1398	858	8	1878	15491
4485	6083	8141	10349	11747	12605	12613	14391
6083	8141	10349	11747	12605	12613	14491	

5

KEEPING
RECORDS

5.0 KEEPING RECORDS

5.1 REASONS FOR KEEPING ACCURATE RECORDS

5.2 KEEPING YOUR RECORDS

T.6 SALES LEDGER (TABLE)

T.7 PURCHASE LEDGER (TABLE)

T.8 CASHBOOK (TABLE)

5.3 BANK RECONCILIATION

5.4 PROFIT AND LOSS ACCOUNT

5.0 <u>KEEPING RECORDS</u>

Whilst your cashflow forecast reflects your best estimate of how your business will perform over the forthcoming period, it is the records you keep that will tell you how you are actually doing on a monthly, weekly or even daily basis. You probably know already that for tax purposes you must keep all your business receipts – and you may have been told that it's OK just to keep them in a shoe box or similar and present them to your bookkeeper or accountant at the end of the year to do your tax returns. But doing this and nothing else will cost you money. It will cost you because you will have to pay your bookkeeper to sort out your mess; it will cost you because you probably won't have much idea of whether all your customers have paid you all they owe; it will cost you if you have to borrow money in order to cover your future debts and it will cost you because you will have no idea as to whether the level of business you are achieving is enough to cover all your expenses.

Creating unnecessary costs for yourself does not make good business sense and could mean that you will soon join the 55% of small businesses that fail in the first year. Don't muddle through – that's no way to do business – instead start by setting up a few simple records and get used to using this information to see how your business is doing and plan for the future.

REASONS FOR
5.1 ## KEEPING ACCURATE RECORDS

A word about HM Revenue and Customs (HMRC) – what they demand and how you will be taxed.

i) Registering with HMRC
When you first start in business you must register with the HMRC within 3 months – under pain of £100 penalty. See their website at http://www. hmrc.gov.uk/selfemployed/register-selfemp.htm or phone the helpline on 0845 915 4515. You can complete a registration form online and you will be asked for your National Insurance number and the name of your business. You may just use your own name if you haven't thought of a separate business name.

ii) Accounting records
All businesses are required by law to keep what the law describes as proper and adequate financial records relating to it and retain these for six years. Even though as a sole trader you do not have to submit your accounts with your Self Assessment tax return you do have to be able to back up your figures if required.

HMRC will also expect you to keep all business records, including bank statements, cheque stubs and paying-in books, mileage records and capital items bought for the business. Keep all business transactions separate from personal transactions by opening a bank account purely for your business. You will also need to keep a record of stock on hand at the accounting date, e.g. 5 April.

iii) <u>The accounting period</u>
You must decide on your 'accounting year' and this can be any date you choose. Regardless of when they start business, many people choose to match their accounting date to the end of the tax year, 5 April (mainly because it simplifies their understanding of how the tax system works). If you make this choice then your first year of business will start on the date you began business and end on 5 April. Each following year it will run from 6th April-5 April.

iv) <u>Calculating profit</u>
As a self-employed person you pay tax on your profits and so for each accounting period or year, you will need to prepare accounts for your business. These accounts will summarise your sales, your variable costs and your fixed costs (and in the first year your start-up costs) so as to arrive at your business profit. One very important point to note is that, because these accounts must show what you have earned, they may include sales for which you have not yet received payment and costs which you have not yet paid.

(This is different to your cashflow & cashbook when you do not show an amount until the money is received).

For tax purposes, only allowable business expenses – costs incurred for the sole purpose of earning business profits – should be included in your costs (your own 'drawings' are not counted as an allowable expense and so cannot be deducted). Where expenses relate to both business and personal use only the business element is allowable. So, for example, if your office is a room in your house, your rent, rates, lighting and heating bills should be split and part of them designated as a business cost according to what proportion of your accommodation is used solely for business purposes

If you have bought any large capital items such as machinery or vehicles, or spent money on such items as the purchase or alteration of business premises these are not included as a business expense but recorded separately as assets of the business. For tax purposes you can claim an Annual Investment Allowance or Capital Allowance which will reduce your taxable profit. (See http://www.hmrc.gov.uk/incometax/relief-self-emp.htm for details of allowable & non-allowable expenses.) You may need to ask a reputable accountant to prepare these accounts if you do not know how to do it yourself – don't forget to include the cost of this help in your fixed cost estimates and budgets.

v) <u>Income tax</u>

As a self-employed person, income tax is payable on the profit your business makes, not the amount of money you take out of the business for your personal needs and use. You have to pay tax on the profit your business makes over a certain level. That level is known as your personal allowance – for 2010/11 this was £6,475. You pay tax only on profit above this amount. In 2010/11 you would have paid 20% on profit from £6,476 – £37,400 and 40% tax on profit over £47,000 per yr.

vi) <u>National Insurance</u>

As a self-employed person you will normally pay Class 2 National Insurance at a fixed rate of £2.40 per week (2010/2011) AND Class 4 NIC of 8% if your profits are above the lower profit limit – £5715 for 2010/2011.

vii) <u>Paying tax</u>

HMRC issues SA316 – Notice to Complete a Tax Return – as soon as the tax year starts on 6 April. You can complete your return online or do it on paper using the records you have kept throughout the year. You must file your return by 31 October if completed on paper or by the following 31st January if online. Either way you must pay the balance of any tax and Class 4 National Insurance you owe by 31 January and at the same time make your first payment on account for the following tax year. You must pay your second payment on account by 31 July.

It is a very good idea to put some money aside each month in order to have funds to pay your tax bill when it is due. Don't neglect this or the tax bill may come as a nasty surprise just when you thought you were doing OK! As a general rule put aside 25% (1/4) of your profits each month into a separate account for tax and NI purposes.

5.2 KEEPING YOUR RECORDS

Tax returns won't be a problem if you keep some simple records. There are three basic sets of information you will need (if you employ staff you will also need a wages book):

- A record of your sales – known as the sales ledger.

- A record of your purchases – known as the purchase ledger.
- The cash book.

A 'ledger' simply means a book where you keep a record of your financial accounts.

- <u>Sales ledger and purchase ledger</u>
You will use these two books to record all the work you have undertaken for which you will be paid and all the expenses you have incurred. These books will provide you with the information you need to do your tax return and your profit and loss statement.

i) <u>Sales ledger</u>
Once you have made a sale issue a numbered invoice and keep a copy. All invoices should show the following information:

- INVOICE.
- Date of the invoice.
- A reference number e.g. 001/10.
- Your business name and address.
- Name and address of the customer you are invoicing.
- A clear description of what you are charging for.
- When the goods or service were provided.
- The amount(s) being charged (net of VAT+VAT

amount = Gross amount if Vat registered).
• Your signature.

File the invoices you have issued in a ring binder in date order with the oldest at the back. If you make any cash sales then issue a numbered receipt and record and file these in the same way. Enter the details in your sales ledger as soon as you have completed the work and issued the invoice.

An extract from an example Sales ledger for 'Sam's View' is shown at the end of the chapter (T.6). He is not VAT registered and so does not need to include any figures in the VAT columns. You can have one column for when your issue the invoice and another for when you actually receive the money – that way you can keep tabs on who has not paid you and chase it up! From this example of 'Sam's View' you will see that J Frampton and Soloquest have not yet paid their invoices – and so perhaps need to be reminded.

ii) <u>Purchase ledger</u>
Your purchase ledger records expenses that you have incurred on behalf of your business. You enter the information into the ledger as soon as you have incurred the expenditure and not when you actually pay for the item or service.

Give the invoices you receive a number e.g. P6/P7 and file them in a ring binder in numerical order with the oldest at the back. If they're fiddly, you could use a system whereby you have a plastic wallet for each month; start by labelling April at the back and go through to March. Put each invoice in the appropriate wallet in the ring binder. Enter the details into your purchase ledger following the example given for 'Sam's View'. (See T.7). (If you are VAT registered you should add two further columns to show expenditure net of VAT and VAT).

Sam has decided that his main budget areas for expenditure are likely to be:

• Photographic supplies.
• Fuel and travel expenses.
• Marketing and Advertising.
• Rent and rates.
• Telephones and stationery.

He has drawn up a separate column for each in his purchase ledger so that he can keep an eye on how much he is spending in each area and at the end of every month he can compare his expenditure against his budget and cashflow estimate for that month.

This is a good way to do business. At the outset of the year you should have decided on your main budget areas i.e. where your main costs are likely to be and how much you are likely to spend in each area. Draw up columns in your purchase ledger to record amounts spent under each budget heading. This information will also help you with your tax return as these costs will be allowable expenses and you will be able to deduct the amounts you have spent from your taxable income. As with 'Sam's View' you should add another column for any other expenses e.g. Contractor Services. Additionally, you could add a final column detailing your personal drawings. That way you have a complete record of all your business expenses.

iii) <u>Cashbook</u>
Record amounts in your cashbook once your invoices are paid (income) or when you make a payment (expenditure). To keep these records you could use a cashbook with Income on the left hand side and Expenditure on the right and total up and rule off at the end of every month. Alternatively, set up your own pages on a computer, using Excel, or use a readymade accounting package. You must decide which is best for you.

Your cashbook is your final record of all money

coming into and going out of your business. It also records what you pay into the bank, what you take out of it and your petty cash. Below is an example of an extract from a cashbook for 'Sam's View'.

Sam has made the payments shown in the Table. You will note from his purchase ledger that he has incurred other expenditure, e.g. he has received an invoice for a mail shot (P9) and one for his supplies (P10), which is not shown in his cashbook because he has not yet issued a cheque or made a card payment for this expenditure. When he does he will enter the amounts into his cashbook.

Your cashbook should help you to work out how much cash you have and whether your payments are exceeding your receipts. If you have a lot of outstanding debtors on your sales ledger you should take steps to make sure they pay before you find yourself in a cash crisis.

T.6 SALES LEDGER

Customer details	Invoice number /10	Date of invoice	Net of VAT total	VAT	Gross total	Date invoice paid (transferred to cash book)
J Frampton	018	26/4/10			390.00	
P Floweth	019	1/5/10			325.00	7/6/10
P Floweth	020	3/5/10			300.00	11/6/10
J Goulding	021	3/5/10			600.00	11/6/10
Soloquest	022	6/5/10			125.00	
J Brown	023	14/5/10			425.00	7/6/10

T.7 **PURCHASE LEDGER**

Date	Invoice no.	Details	Purchases / Expenditure	
			Supplies	Petrol / diesel and travel
1/6/10	P6	Rent		
3/6/10	P7	Contractor services		
5/6/10	P8	Fuel		60.00
6/6/10	P9	Mail shot		
11/6/10	P10	Photographic Supplies	310.00	
12/6/10	P11	Mobile phone		
15/6/10	P12	Stationery		
16/6/10	P13	Fuel		60.00
17/6/10	P14	Film	15.00	
20/6/10	P15	Car repairs		
24/6/10	P16	BT		
29/6/10	P17	Contractor services		
30/6/10	P18	Fuel		70.00
TOTAL			325.00	190.00

				Date Paid
Marketing and advertising	Rent and rates	Telephones and office costs	Other allowable expenses	
	120.00			1/6/10
			200.00	30/6/10
				5/6/10
125.00				
		35.00		12/6/10
		22.40		
				16/6/10
			65.00	20/6/10
		15.00		
			145.98	30/6/10
				30/6/10
125.00	120.00	72.40	410.98	

T.8 CASHBOOK

INCOME					
Date	Invoice no.	Details	Type	Amount (£)	Date paid into bank a/c
7/6/10	023	J Brown	Cheque 012336	425.00	10/6/10
10/6/10	019	P Floweth	Credit transfer	325.00	10 /6/10
11 /6/10	-	Interest on investment account		50.00	11 /6/10
11 /6/10	021	J Goulding	Cheque 006782	600.00	13 /6/10
14 /6/10	020	P Floweth	Credit transfer	300.00	14 /6/10

EXPENDITURE					
Date	Ref. no	Supplier / payee	Type	Amount (£)	Petty cash
1 /6/10	P6	R Briggs	Cheque 002564	120.00	
3 /6/10	P7	S Jones	Cheque 002565	200.00	
5 /6/10	P8	Shell	Card	60.00	
15 /6/10	P 12	Viking	Card	22.40	
20 /6/10	PC				50.00

5.3 BANK RECONCILIATION

Make sure that you receive a bank statement for your business bank account once a month. Make time each month to check that all monies that you have paid into your bank account are recorded and that all cheques that you have written or other payments that you have made are also shown. There may be some discrepancies, for example, if you have paid for something by cheque which has not yet been presented by the receiver or if a cheque you have paid in has not yet gone through or has 'bounced'.

To double check that your cash book and bank account agree you should do a bank reconciliation as soon as you have your bank statement to hand for that month. These are the steps to take:

i) Note the end of month balance as per bank statement.
ii) ADD deposits you have made that are not shown on the statement.
iii) DEDUCT payments that you have made that are not shown on the bank statement.

Is the final figure the same as your cashbook? If, 'yes' then you have reconciled your bank account with your cashbook. Great! If 'no' then investigate further. For example, there may be bank charges on your bank statement that will not be included in your cashbook or you may have received interest into your bank account that you did not know about. Add the receipts to, or deduct the payments from, your cashbook balance.

5.4 PROFIT AND LOSS ACCOUNT

Your cashflow forecast is a prediction of how you think your business will perform over a certain period and once you have received income or made expenditure you update it with the information. However, it is not an accurate picture of the value of your business over this period as there will be work that you have done for which you have not yet been paid, or costs that you have incurred that you have not yet met. Unlike your cashflow, your profit and loss calculations refer only to work done in that particular period.

Once you take these into account, together with an estimation of the amount of depreciation on your capital items, then you will have a much truer picture of the profit or losses that your business is making. Providing you keep accurate sales and purchase ledgers and a cashbook your bookkeeper or accountant will be able to draw up a profit and loss statement for you.

6

YOUR BUSINESS PLAN

6.0 <u>YOUR BUSINESS PLAN</u>

Once you have carried out your market research, decided on how you will market your business, estimated your budgets and your cashflow and decided how you are going to 'do' business, you should put it altogether into your business plan. Your business plan will be a description of everything we have talked about in this book as it relates to your business. In it you should explain what you want to achieve and how you are going to achieve it.

If you are applying for outside funding or a loan your plan must cover all of the aspects in reasonable detail; if the amount you need to borrow is substantial then you will need greater detail with complete financial projections.

However, for your own purposes writing a simple business plan to start with will help you think about what you hope to achieve and how to achieve it. It will assist you in putting the building blocks in place so that you go in the right direction, don't waste money on false leads or fantasies and get the right experience and training in order to create a successful business and then grow that business.

6.1 <u>WHY HAVE A BUSINESS PLAN?</u>

There are two very good reasons for taking time to write a business plan:

i) It will help you gather your thoughts and bring together in one place all the different pieces of information you have. As you write it you must be truthful with yourself and analyse whether you really do have a solid business idea. Take action to put right any shortfalls in your plan.

ii) If you need to apply to a funding body, such as a bank or other organisation, for a loan for the business they will want to see your business plan. They will only lend to businesses that stand a good chance of being able to repay the loan, so your business plan must convince them of this.

Statistics show that over half of small businesses in the UK fold within the first year. You do not need to be one of these! The main reasons for failure are reported to be:

- <u>Lack of planning and research</u> – working through a business plan will help ensure you do not fail for these reasons. You must be sure there is a market for your product or service and that you can sell at a profit.
- <u>Cashflow</u> – late payments by customers threaten the future of your business. However, by keeping

accurate records – a sales ledger, a purchase ledger and a cashbook – and updating your cashflow at the end of every month, you need not fall into this trap.

- <u>Marketing</u> – many small businesses do little or no marketing and when they do advertise it may not reach those customers who are likely to buy the product or services. A simple marketing plan will help you 'sell' the benefits of your business to the right customers at the right time and in the right place.

- <u>General management skills</u> – you may not have all the skills you need to run a business and if you do not recognise this then you may be incapable of managing your businesses. If you find yourself in this situation either acquire the skills or knowledge yourself (remember there are a lot of free short business-related courses on offer) or find someone who can do the work for you, for example, a bookkeeper. Whichever solution you choose, don't ignore the issue.

The bottom line for many sole traders is that they lack funds to enable them to carry out their work, however, by paying attention to the above areas you can avoid the pitfalls. By grasping and understanding the reasons for failure you can take steps to avoid them and improve your chances of success. You can view sample business plans online. See www.bplans.co.uk/sample_business_plans.

T.9 TEMPLATE FOR A BUSINESS PLAN

An example of the headings you could use for your plan are given below (T. 9) together with the main points you should include under each heading. You will see that just about everything has already been covered somewhere in the book.

BUSINESS NAME:	
BUSINESS ADDRESS:	
TELEPHONE NUMBERS:	
EMAIL ADDRESS:	
WEBSITE:	
1	BUSINESS DESCRIPTION (Describe:)
1.1	Who you are, the product(s) or service(s) you are offering, your main customers
1.2	Why there is a need for your service
1.3	What will give you an edge over your competition – your business model

2	PERSONAL SKILLS AND EXPERIENCE (Describe:)
2.1	Why you want to run your own business
2.2	Relevant employment or self-employment experience, including voluntary work or projects
2.3	Relevant qualifications, licenses, certificates and training
2.4	Any notable achievements you are proud of which will help you in your business (think broadly)
2.5	Any personal skills gaps you have identified and your plans to bridge these gaps, with dates
3	MARKET RESEARCH (Describe:)
3.1	What market research you have carried out AND what you discovered from your customers from this
3.2	The size of your market, whether you have different sets of customers (segments) that you will need to treat differently and how you will grow the market, including trends
3.3	Your competition. Where the main competition will come from and how you plan to compete. You could include a SWOT analysis of your competition and use this to explain the main areas where you plan to compete
4	MARKETING PLAN (Describe:)
4.1	The main benefits you will be selling
4.2	How you plan to get you message out to your customers e.g. word of mouth, internet, telephone, leaflets, car stickers, newspaper advertising etc. Give a timescale for these different actions
4.3	Marketing costs – your annual budget. (Include as an appendix with other budgets)
4.4	What you hope to achieve from your marketing e.g. planned numbers of new customers, selling more to current customers and how you will monitor success, e.g. keep a record of referrals

5	OPERATIONAL DETAILS (Describe:)
5.1	Where you will be based and confirmation that you hold any licences or have landlords / mortgage companies permissions to use the premises. What facilities you will need / already have
5.2	Your suppliers and supplier arrangements (if applicable)
5.3	Delivery to customers – delivery time and method
5.4	How you will be paid and how you will pay suppliers. Time lags?
5.5	Legal requirements – confirm what insurances you will need, describe health and safety requirements, patents applied for if applicable
6	COSTS AND PRICING (Describe:)
6.1	What you will charge for your product(s) or service(s)
6.2	How you arrived at these figures e.g. based on what competitors are charging? Explain your position
7	SALES ANALYSIS (Describe:)
7.1	Expected value of sales in an average month, good month, poor month. Explain how you arrived at these figures e.g. seasonal variations
7.2	Cashflow – Explain any anomalies or uncertainties in your cashflow and refer to your cashflow at Appendix C
7.3	Your breakeven position. Do the sums
8	MILESTONES
	Include any milestones important to you here
9	APPENDICES
A	Budget
B	Personal survival income
C	Cashflow forecast

6.2 EXECUTIVE SUMMARY

Once you have written your business plan you should prepare a short summary of it which you attach to the front of the plan. This is so that any busy executives, such as your bank manager, can assess very quickly whether or not your business is one in which they might be interested. You can summarise any figures in this section without explaining these.

Follow this format giving about a paragraph on each section:

- What is your business and who are your customers?
- What is important to your customers – that you will be able to offer?
- What is the size of your market and how will you meet this demand?
- Your skills and experience that will ensure success. (Use this section to impress the reader about your abilities and enthusiasm to succeed).
- How big is your market and by how much might it grow?
- What profits do you forecast?
- What are your longer term aims (or your vision for the business).
- Financial summary – how much you have already invested in the business and, if applying for funding.

- How much money you need and when will this be repaid?

6.3 STAYING LEGAL

Although it is easy to start up as a sole trader there are some things you must do. Work through this checklist of the main areas you need to think about.

T. 10 LEGAL CHECKLIST

TOPIC	CHECKED
Register with HMRC – you must register with HMRC (www.hmrc.gov.uk) for tax and national Insurance purposes as soon as you start to trade.	
Licences – Some types of business require licences, for example if you are working with children, if you sell alcohol, or are dealing with food. Check with your Local Authority, Trade or Professional Association to make sure you have the required licences to do business.	
Your trading name – if you intend to operate as a sole trader using a name other than your own, there is a legal requirement for the name and address of the owner to be displayed at your business premises and on your business stationery. The Companies Act 2006 sets out the requirements regarding the use of business names. This part of the Act will apply to you	

if you use a name that is not your normal surname (with or without initials). For example if a person called Jenny Smith is a photographer and trades as Jenny Smith or J. Smith she is not affected by the Act. However, if she trades as Jenny Smith Photographer then the Act applies. You can get free advice on business names from Companies House (See www.companieshouse.gov.uk).	
Insurances – some insurances are compulsory for businesses. The best way to check which insurances you might need is to go to the Business Link web site and answer the questions in the interactive tool. See www.businesslink.gov.uk and click on 'Finances and Grants' and then 'Insurances' , 'Get the right insurance for your business'. Some insurances you should consider are:	
Employers' liability – If you employ staff you should check out the Health and Safety Executive's 'Employers' Guide' (See www.hse.gov.uk/pubns/hse40.pdf).	
Motor insurance – check with you insurance company that your insurance covers business use. If you use your car or van to transport goods for your business then you will need to buy a separate insurance policy.	
Public liability insurance – covers you if someone sues you for injury to themselves or damage to their property caused in the course of your work.	
Property and stock insurance – check your property insurance to make sure that all machinery, stock, tools, equipment etc are covered. Look for an 'all risks' clause.	
Professional indemnity – this is relevant if you provide advice such as accountants and business advisers. It covers legal liability for professional errors or omissions.	

Health and safety (H&S) – there are several areas of H&S legislation that apply to businesses, no matter what their size. If you employ staff you must be especially attentive to ensuring they operate in a safe working environment. This duty also extends to visitors to the workplace such as customers and suppliers. The H&S Executive website has lots of useful information and fact sheets and you can order a Starter Pack from them. See www.hse.gov.uk/business/pack.htm or call 0845 345 0055.	
Data protection – the gathering and holding of personal data is tightly regulated. It includes rules such as ensuring that you have a person's consent before processing information about them, only keeping relevant, accurate and timely information and ensuring that it is stored securely. These principles apply to all databases, whether computerized or manual. If you keep a computer database you may also be required to notify the Information Commissioner so that your name can be added to the public register of data controllers. For further information see www.ico.gov.uk or call 01625 545745.	
Intellectual property – patents, trademarks, copyright and designs – Most sole traders need not be concerned with obtaining legal protection for their product or idea. However, if you do wish to protect some aspect of your business then you should investigate further. Some intellectual property rights are automatic, whilst others require a registration process before they become legally enforceable. If registration is required make sure that you register your IP concept before you disclose any details publicly. Always keep records of your work and add your name and date to these. As IP registration is complicated you will need the services of a registered patent or trademark agent to ensure that your work is legally protected. See www.ipo.gov.uk for more information.	

<u>Business Link</u> has an online regulation checklist that you can work through to find out which regulations are likely to apply to you. See **www.busineslink.gov.uk** Click the 'do it online' tab and choose the regulation checklist.	
<u>Solicitors</u> – you may decide that you would like some legal advice to help with such things as contracts, offering personal guarantees, health and safety law, debt collection, product protection and so on. You could start by going to the Lawyers for Business website: **www.contactlaw.co.uk**. Experienced staff can offer you free advice over the phone and put you in touch with the right solicitor for your needs from their register of solicitors.	
<u>Opening a business bank account</u> – you should keep your business finances separate from your personal money. The British Bankers Association offers a 'Business Account Finder' service for small businesses. See **www.bba.org.uk** for further information.	

6.4 <u>LEARN AS YOU GO</u>

Once you're up and running you'll be on a steep learning curve. Within 6 months of starting your business you'll know a huge amount more than you do now. Take time to look over your business plan and adjust your ideas according to what you have learnt. You'll have discovered a lot along the way – so make the most of it and don't stand still.

FINAL WORD

Running your own business will make demands on you and challenge you to do things you probably would avoid if it weren't for the fact that you are now responsible for the success or failure of your business. By putting yourself in this position you may surprise yourself by finding new skills and talents that you weren't previously aware you possessed. Try and recognise where your talents lie and build on them and gain self-confidence from using and developing them. Of course, there will be areas where you are weak – but recognising where these areas are is a skill in itself – no one is good at everything, but the most successful people realise what they need help with and then go and find that help.

May I wish you every success with your business.

Lightning Source UK Ltd.
Milton Keynes UK
UKOW051816260112

186140UK00001B/3/P